MIGHTY MACHINES

Graders

by Mary Lindeen

BLASTOFF! READERS

BELLWETHER MEDIA · MINNEAPOLIS, MN

Note to Librarians, Teachers, and Parents:

Blastoff! Readers are carefully developed by literacy experts and combine standards-based content with developmentally-appropriate text.

Level 1 provides the most support through repetition of high-frequency words, light text, predictable sentence patterns, and strong visual support.

Level 2 offers early readers a bit more challenge through varied simple sentences, increased text load, and less repetition of high frequency words.

Level 3 advances early-fluent readers toward fluency through increased text and concept load, less reliance on visuals, longer sentences, and more literary language.

Level 4 builds reading stamina by providing more text per page, increased use of punctuation, greater variation in sentence patterns, and increasingly challenging vocabulary.

Level 5 encourages children to move from "learning to read" to "reading to learn" by providing even more text, varied writing styles, and less familiar topics.

Whichever book is right for your reader, Blastoff! Readers are the perfect books to build confidence and encourage a love of reading that will last a lifetime!

This edition first published in 2008 by Bellwether Media.

No part of this publication may be reproduced in whole or in part without written permission of the publisher. For information regarding permission, write to Bellwether Media Inc., Attention: Permissions Department, Post Office Box 1C, Minnetonka, MN 55345-9998.

Library of Congress Cataloging-in-Publication Data
Lindeen, Mary.
  Graders / by Mary Lindeen.
    p. cm. — (Mighty machines) (Blastoff! readers)
Summary: "Simple text and supportive images introduce young readers to graders.
Intended for students in kindergarten through third grade"–Provided by publisher.
  Includes bibliographical references and index.
  ISBN-13: 978-1-60014-118-8 (hardcover : alk. paper)
  ISBN-10: 1-60014-118-8 (hardcover : alk. paper)
  1. Graders (Earthmoving machinery)—Juvenile literature. I. Title.

TA725.L56 2008
621.8'65–dc22

2007009767

Contents

What Is a Grader?   4

Parts of a Grader   8

Graders at Work   16

Glossary   22

To Learn More   23

Index   24

A grader is a big machine. It scrapes the ground and makes it flat.

Now a road
can be built
on flat ground.

A grader has
a long **blade**.

blade

Graders push dirt and rocks out of the way.

A grader has a **cab**.
A driver sits in the cab.

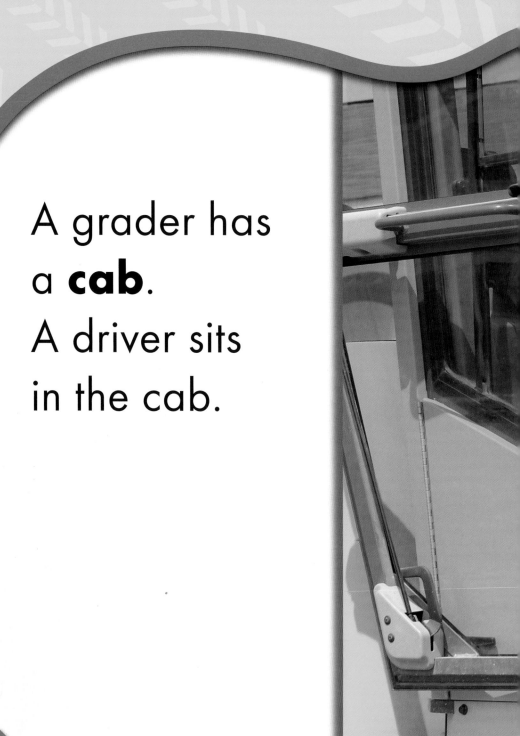

A grader has an **engine** in the back.

This grader
pushes snow.

This grader
flattens
the top
of a hill.

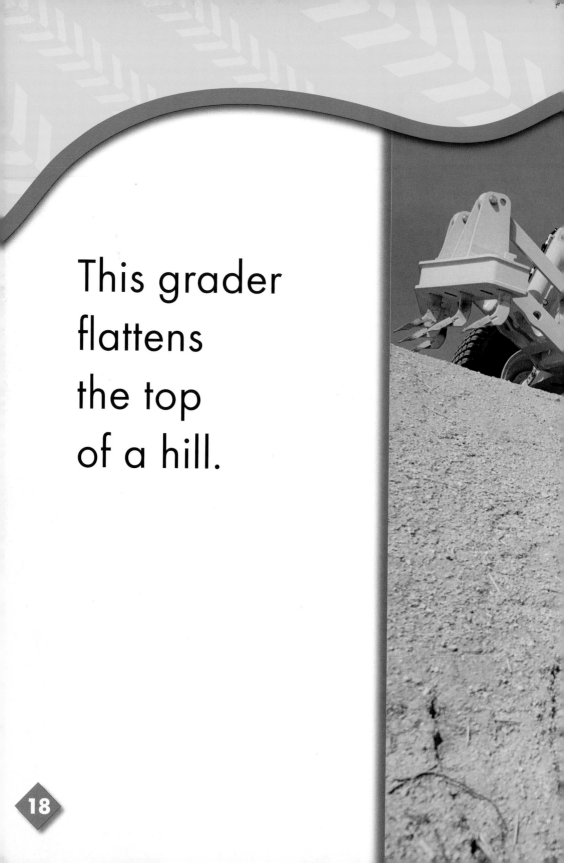

This grader
can move
a lot of dirt.

Glossary

blade—the broad, flat part of a grader used to scrape and push things on the ground

cab—a place where the driver sits

engine—a machine that can move a vehicle

To Learn More

AT THE LIBRARY

Adams, Georgie. *Highway Builders*. Toronto, ON: Annick, 2001.

Blum, Mark. *Big Trucks and Diggers in 3-D*. San Francisco, Calif.: Chronicle, 2001.

Zemlicka, Shannon. *From Rock to Road*. Minneapolis, Minn.: Lerner, 2004.

ON THE WEB

Learning more about mighty machines is as easy as 1, 2, 3.

1. Go to www.factsurfer.com

2. Enter "mighty machines" into search box.

3. Click the "Surf" button and you will see a list of related web sites.

With factsurfer.com, finding more information is just a click away.

Index

back, 14
blade, 8
cab, 12
dirt, 10, 20
driver, 12
engine, 14
ground, 4, 6
machine, 4
road, 6
rocks, 10
snow, 16

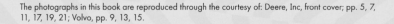

The photographs in this book are reproduced through the courtesy of: Deere, Inc, front cover; pp. 5, 7, 11, 17, 19, 21; Volvo, pp. 9, 13, 15.